3 Keys to Defeating Unconscious Bias

3 KEYS TO DEFEATING UNCONSCIOUS BIAS

WATCH, THINK, ACT

SONDRA THIEDERMAN PH.D.

To order additional copies of this book or for information about other products and
services, contact us by phone at
619-583-4478
or by e-mail at
stphd@thiederman.com.
Or you can visit www.thiederman.com.

© 2015 Sondra Thiederman Ph.D.

Cross-Cultural Communications
4585 Forty-Eighth Street
San Diego, CA 92115
619-583-4478
stphd@thiederman.com

ISBN: 0964497727
ISBN 13: 9780964497726
Library of Congress Control Number: 2015906855
Cross-Cultural Communications, San Diego, CA
Printed in the United States of America

*To my sister, Susan Campbell Swan, who knows I'll always be there to help
with that squeak in the stairs*

CONTENTS

INTRODUCTION

WHY WATCH, THINK, ACT?

Don't you just hate powerlessness? Speaking strictly for me, the sense that I can't control something is one of my least favorite feelings.

Let's face it: there are many things in life that we can't control, but lucky for us, bias isn't one of them. In fact, there's plenty we can do about our biases, and that's where WATCH, THINK, and ACT come in.

You'll learn more about what you are being asked to WATCH, what to THINK about, and how to ACT in the pages to come, but here is a brief overview to give you an idea of where we are headed.

> WATCH your thoughts, your past experiences, and your actions for signs of unconscious bias.

> THINK about the people you know, about how you would feel were a bias directed at you, about your values, and about pausing long enough to get your bias out of the way.

> ACT as if your bias doesn't exist, and to identify common ground.

As you will see, each of these verbs has a purpose. WATCH will move your bias from your unconscious to your conscious awareness. THINK and ACT will give you control of the bias and, very possibly, eliminate it altogether.

Bias is a labor-saving device. It enables you to form an opinion without having to dig up the facts.

Anonymous

WHAT IS A BIAS?

"My sister drives me crazy. Every time we go to dinner, she wants Mexican food. Her bias sure limits where we get to eat."

"Joe has always had a bias for outdoor activities. Not sure where it came from, but every time I turn around, he seems to be off skiing or something."

"Blue, blue, blue. Talk about having a bias for a color! Everything Nancy wears is one shade of blue or another. Even the walls of her room are painted something she calls 'periwinkle.'"

Clearly, these are not the kinds of biases we are talking about in this book. *Bias* is a rich English word that has several uses. There's the idea of cutting something like fabric at a forty-five-degree angle, which is called "cutting on the bias." There's an effort to sway someone's opinion ("The lawyer is trying to bias the jury") and a preference for one thing over another ("My sister has a strong bias for Mexican food").

And then there's *bias* as we are using it in this book:

A bias is an inflexible, positive or negative, often unconscious belief about a particular **category of people**.

Notice the bolded phrase "category of people." These three words cut to the heart of the kind of bias we are addressing here. We are not talking about a preference for one person based on what you know about him or her as an individual. Instead, we are concerned with an attitude toward an entire group of people. It doesn't matter what defines that group—it can be age, gender, occupation, nationality, ethnicity, race, or any other of dozens of criteria.

The key to what makes a belief a bias is the concept of *all*: "All women are nurturing." Or, "All Asians are good at math." On the other hand, it is not a bias if the belief is flexible: "Some generation X workers change jobs a lot." Or, "Some Italians are good cooks."

The simplest way to conceive of a bias is as the small voice inside each of us that, upon meeting a stranger, whispers, "I've known someone similar to you before, so I know what you are like."

You'll notice too that, according to our definition, not all biases are about negative characteristics. It is, you see, just as biased to apply a desirable characteristic to every member of a group ("All Asians are good at technology") as an undesirable one ("All white people are racist"). The common denominator between negative and positive biases is that both involve an inflexible belief applied to all members of a group; in turn, both prevent the observer from accurately seeing the person in front of them.

Another—more lighthearted—way to look at bias is to paraphrase nineteenth-century journalist Ambrose Bierce:

"A bias is a vagrant opinion without visible means of support."

WHERE THE "UNCONSCIOUS" COMES IN

I remember that as a child, I would look up at the night sky and try to imagine what existed at that point in the universe where the stars ended; at ten years old, I was trying to imagine nothingness. Although there was a certain masochistic pleasure in the uneasy feeling that this imagining sparked in my adolescent brain, ultimately pursuing such grand questions is inclined to drive people crazy.

I feel the same way about trying to fathom the unconscious mind. Does it have substance? Can it be located? Can we take a picture of it? "No" is the disconcerting answer to each of these questions. That doesn't, however, mean that the unconscious—and the biases it shelters—doesn't have a profound impact on the decisions we make, the things we say, and how we live our lives.

But how do these biases end up lodged in our unconscious in the first place? Biases, as pointed out by Mahzarin Banaji and Anthony G. Greenwald in their book, *Blindspot: Hidden Biases of Good People*, are formed through collecting bits of knowledge that we associate with something else. As Banaji and Greenwald put it, "The mind is an automatic association-making machine." (Banaji & Greenwald 2013)

Unfortunately, this association game doesn't apply merely to inanimate objects (we see a couch and associate it with comfort or watching television); it also happens with groups of people with whom we associate a particular characteristic. The question then becomes, "Where do these bits of knowledge come from?"

The simple answer is that they come from everywhere. We stumble on them during casual conversations with those who pass on a rumor they heard about a particular group. They hurtle at us out of the screens of television sets and computers and movie theaters where the depictions of people are riddled with exaggeration and caricature. Perhaps most insidious, biases are whispered in our ears by parents and teachers and the society as a whole, often so subtly that they enter our unconscious completely unnoticed. This wouldn't be so bad if the bits and pieces were always accurate, but they're not—and that's where the problems begin.

THE PROBLEMS BIASES CREATE FOR US

Truth be told, these maligned little chunks of knowledge—our biases—originally served a function. They allowed us to make decisions quickly about who was an enemy and who a friend. That primitive function, however, has long outlived its usefulness. Like my now useless appendix that, if infected, can kill me, biases today do far more harm than good.

For one thing, biases do harm to the person who harbors them. As we've seen, biases prevent us from seeing people accurately. Because of that inaccuracy, we are at risk of making all kinds of errors—errors that compromise success in both our personal and professional lives.

Here are just a few examples of the kinds of havoc biases can wreak:

- Jeff got in trouble with his boss because he never offered travel opportunities to the mothers on his team. Turns out he had a bias that said, "Women with children are reluctant to travel for work." Rather than ask the qualified mothers what they really wanted, he made an assumption that came back to haunt him.

- Sally lost the opportunity to make new friends because her bias informed her, "People who are gay have completely different values than I do." As a result, she failed to befriend her new neighbors only to learn years later that the couple shared many of her points of view and interests.

- Joe had difficulty getting along with colleagues at work. The problem was that Joe's bias distorted his view of the younger people around him. Every time he saw a colleague under thirty, he assumed the person was less hardworking than he and, worse, apt to quit at any moment.

Sadly, examples like these are just the very tiny tip of the iceberg of the problems our biases create for us.

THE PROBLEMS BIASES CREATE FOR OTHERS

On the other side of the equation, what about the damage done to the targets of bias? Most obviously, it is painful to live in an environment in which people assume you are a certain way solely because of the group to which you belong. Whether that target is a person with a disability whom we assume to be helpless because of his or her wheelchair or a black man to be athletic because of his race, the feeling is one of being negated as an individual and, all too often, of being deprived of opportunity.

There are other problems too that bias creates. Take a thing called the "stereotype threat," for example. The stereotype threat is the fear felt by the target of a bias that he or she might do something to inadvertently confirm the negative thoughts about them. That is, I'm sure you'd agree, a horrible way to live. Imagine, for example, a person under thirty who knows her colleagues believe, "All young people aren't experienced enough to have good ideas."

Some people under these circumstances might decide to defy the bias and feel compelled to speak up in order to prove it wrong. Others, understandably, might choose instead to keep their thoughts to themselves so as to avoid the risk of inadvertently confirming the stereotype. None of us, after all, always come up with our best ideas, and there are days when we are off our game.

Then there's what's called "internalization." Internalization is what happens when the target of the bias actually believes what the bias says. Think about yourself for example. Are there any inflexible beliefs about your group that, at least at some point in your life, you came to believe?

I can't know what demographic group you are a part of, but I do know mine: white, baby boomer, female. I grew up in the 1950s and '60s when women were still stereotyped as "naturally" not designed to be good at business. Although my parents were more enlightened than most and my environment fairly sophisticated, I still bought into that bias, and as a consequence, it took me years to gain confidence in the world of business plans, marketing strategies and—truth be told—budgets.

Most of us are good people, and, as good people, it is awful to know that any bias we might have is negatively impacting not only us but others as well. Luckily, there's a lot we can do to short-circuit these inflexible beliefs and bring much of this destruction to an end.

THERE'S A LOT WE CAN DO ABOUT BIAS

The game that the brain plays of linking bits of knowledge to particular groups is a natural feature of our unconscious. Just because it is "natural," however, does not mean it can't be controlled—and often even defeated.

Think about the other "natural" things humankind used to engage in and perhaps never dreamt could or should be controlled. We've learned to show self-control, for example, over personal hygiene and the kinds of things we believe are appropriate to do in public. Let's face it: that restraint is in a very real sense "unnatural," but we have achieved it anyway.

Another phenomenon that is intrinsic to human nature is the impulse to categorize groups. After all, we've had to do this for our survival. With limited weaponry, technology, and communication skills, what else could we do but assume that all members of another tribe were to be feared? This inflexible belief is the grandfather of all bias.

Fortunately, times and survival conditions have changed. Today we have more control over our environments, and along with that control comes the luxury to defeat our biases.

That is where the skills in this handbook come in. By becoming aware of our unconscious biases, by using our thoughts to weaken them, and by behaving in ways that run counter to what the biases tell us is real, we truly can get them under control and out of our way.

DO YOU REALLY WANT TO TAKE THIS ON?

Does this sound kind of scary? I'll admit the thought of digging into the unconscious to pull out hidden biases may be daunting. After all, what if you find something?

Well, if you do find something, join the club. Everybody has biases—I sure do—and guess what?

Biases do not make you a bad person!

Biases are just a way of coping with a complex, stressful, and ever-changing world. Yes, biases are bad because they block the ability to see others accurately, but most of the people who hold biases are multifaceted human beings, complete with virtues, sins, and everything in between. What makes a biased person bad, or at least unwise, is refusing to identify the bias and accept responsibility for getting it under control.

Think of it like this: What this book really amounts to is a means for uncovering and dealing with buried attitudes that are interfering with your ability to make good decisions, to treat people with respect, and to form fruitful relationships. When you look at it that way, maybe the process isn't so scary after all.

So let's get started.

We need to move our responses to others out of our guts and into our minds.

Jennifer James
Urban Cultural Anthropologist

Key #1

WATCH

THE WISDOM OF WATCHING

The lucky thing about biases is that even the ones lying deep in our unconscious aren't very good at staying hidden. All but the most profoundly buried ones reveal their existence at one time or another. Biases are, after all, attitudes, and all attitudes eventually show themselves in an action or in a thought.

And that's where WATCHing comes in. The purpose of WATCHing is to spot our biases as they waft up from our unconscious. Once that bias is spotted and identified, we then have the power to target it for extinction. Call it "mindfulness," "vigilance," or "self-awareness"; it all boils down to paying attention to what we think and what we do.

WATCH YOUR THOUGHTS AND ASSUMPTIONS

Initially, this instruction to WATCH your thoughts might seem odd— a little like spying on your internal self. In fact, it really is pretty straightforward.

We've all WATCHed our thoughts before. Have you ever been asked to say the first thing that comes to mind when you hear a word like "cat," "house," or "bacon"? You likely responded with "dog," "home," and "eggs."

When you notice the word that comes to mind, you are WATCHing your thoughts. That's all there is to it. We do it all the time. It's just that when it comes to something more substantial than a parlor game (like becoming aware of a bias), we lose sight of how simple and familiar the process is.

I recall the very instant that I became aware of my ability to WATCH my biases. It involved unearthing a bias that until that moment was hiding deep in my unconscious.

This revelation struck as I was returning to my hotel room after doing a presentation at a resort in central California. The room lay just off a balcony that overlooked the hotel's cocktail lounge. As I crossed the balcony, I looked down to see a large group of tourists entering the lounge and dividing themselves among the tiny round tables. I also noticed that the members of the group were quite elderly—most appeared to be in their eighties.

It was just as I saw the group that my previously unconscious bias came hurtling into my brain. It did so in the form of this thought: *Gee, I'm glad I'm not down there with them; those conversations must be boring.*

To this day, I remember my shock. I had no idea—none—that this bias ("Elderly people are boring") was lurking in my unconscious. The bias was certainly not good news. There was, however, a silver lining to that dismal revelation. Namely, I woke up to the fact that it really is possible to spot our biases if only we pay attention and WATCH for them.

Paying attention, though, needs to become a habit, a knee-jerk reaction. We can't count on the brain to naturally notice our responses in the midst of all the stimulation that is perpetually coming at us. To form that habit, we need repetition and practice. Here is a short activity to get you started.

Below you will find a list of words. (**Stop!** Don't look at the list until you are ready to do the exercise.) As you read the list, make a mental note of the first thought—the first assumption—that comes into your mind. OK, go ahead:

- A person in a wheelchair
- An immigrant from Mexico
- A Muslim
- A single mother with three children
- A native of New York City

How you responded to each group isn't the point just now. What matters is that you practiced noticing your first thought.

But how can you know whether that first assumption really is an inflexible bias? Maybe, instead, it is merely what I call a "working generality." Working generalities are different from biases in that they have a very flimsy hold on our thoughts; we give them up easily in the face of contradictory evidence. They are really along the lines of a "first best guess" and are subject to modification without much effort.

In order to tell the difference between a best guess and a bias, subject that first response to what I call the "Bias ID Test." Here are the questions to ask:

1. When I had the first thought, did I have the word "all" in my head? Was there the implication that the characteristic that came to mind applied to every member of the group? If not, it was probably just a flexible working generality.
2. Would I feel the same way about the meaning of this incident if the person were of a different group?" For example, let's say you are observing a new female executive give a presentation. At one point, she begins to pound the table, raise her voice, and pace the platform. Your first thought is this: *Gee, she sure is getting hysterical.*

Now, ask yourself, "If the speaker were a man, would I still have thought him hysterical or, instead, would I have assumed he was merely enthusiastic?" If the answer is "enthusiastic," you probably have a bias on your hands.

3. What do I do when I discover the first assumption was wrong? If you just let it go and change your mind, you are probably fine. If, on the other hand, you become upset and do everything you can to resist the evidence in front of your eyes by saying something like, "This person is an exception to the rule," you are almost certainly in bias territory.

The next step in this bias awareness process is to take the practice of WATCHing your first assumption out into the world. I'll wager that before too long, you'll discover that you have formed a new and very productive habit. Go ahead and give it a try.

Antibias Activity: What Comes to Mind

For the next two weeks, notice and write down in the space below the first thought that comes to mind when you encounter someone from a different group. Once you identify that first assumption, subject it to the Bias ID Test found in this chapter.

WATCH YOUR PAST EXPERIENCES

"WATCH your past experiences" sounds, I realize, suspiciously like time travel. In fact, it is simply another way to bring unconscious biases into conscious awareness.

Biases, you see, are learned in part through our intense experiences with people different from us. By examining those experiences, we can identify any biases the event might have spawned.

I say "intense experiences" because it is those that are most apt to create bias. That intensity, by the way, does not have to be negative.

Positive experiences are just as apt to instill bias. Admittedly, the bias created will be about a positive characteristic, but it is nonetheless a bias—an inflexible belief about a particular category of people.

The idea here is to look back at experiences that have two characteristics:

1. The experience involved an encounter or relationship with a member of a group that was different from your own in some way.
2. The experience had an emotional impact that was either intensely negative or intensely positive.

As I write these words, my mind is skimming for how I would complete this exercise. Varied memories and images are popping into my mind—the Italian family down the street, my black best friend in junior high school, the scary incident at the gas station while in college. I wonder what those experiences tell me about my biases. Hmm...lots to think about.

Antibias Activity: Looking Back

Record in this space three events involving people different from you that were positively or negatively intense enough to possibly create a bias. Record as many details as you can recall. When you are finished, give some thought to what bias each event might have planted in your unconscious.

Event #1

Event #2

Event #3

WATCH YOUR ACTIONS AND DECISIONS

Another way to become aware of our biases is to WATCH our behaviors and the decisions that led to those behaviors. This involves—painful though it may be—thinking back to times you interacted with someone different from you and examining those interactions for bias. These interactions can be at work or in your personal life. Once you've identified some examples, ask yourself these questions—the answers can be most revealing:

- In any of these events, did your actions reflect a preference for one group over another? I don't mean a preference for an individual within the group, but for the group as a whole.
- Did any of these events involve saying something that you now feel was disrespectful to the group involved?
- If you are in a management position, did any of these events involve hiring or promoting one group over another? Considering the demographic mix of qualified candidates,

was the distribution of hires and promotions different than you would have expected it to be?

- Did any of these events involve being "nicer" to one group over another? I'm not talking about being kind to one individual because he or she needed or deserved it but rather treating an entire group more gently than another.
- In any of these incidents, do you recall justifying the actions of the people with whom you identify (the members of your own group), but not those of the other group?
- When thinking back, do you recall ever recounting an incident involving people different from you in which you mentioned a person's demographic category (race, ethnicity, sexual orientation, etc.) when that category had nothing to do with the story? If so, it might just be that you are thinking of that person as a member of a group rather than as an individual.

As you WATCH your decisions, activities, and choices, don't be afraid of what you might find. Remember, biases don't make you a bad person—they make you human. And because you are human, you are capable of change.

Antibias Activity: Keeping Watch

For the next month, WATCH your actions and decisions with respect to people different from you, and subject each interaction to the questions listed above. As you go through this process, try to think of other questions you might ask to unearth a bias.

Watch your thoughts, they become words; watch your words, they become actions; watch your actions, they become habits; watch your habits, they become character; watch your character, for it becomes your destiny.

Frank Outlaw
Late President, Bi-Lo Stores

Key #2

THINK

THE POWER OF THOUGHT

In Key #1, we talked about how to become aware of our biases. Now let's move to how we can manage and defeat biases by using our ability to Think. The fundamental principle here is this:

Logic is power.

The more logic—the more good sense—we bring to the challenge of defeating bias, the more progress we will make. Logic, I am glad to say, is a weapon well designed to defeat the knee-jerk reactions that past experiences and environments have embedded in our unconscious.

THINK ABOUT THE PEOPLE YOU ACTUALLY KNOW

Let's start by Thinking about how many people you **actually know** who conform to your bias. When I say "actually know," I don't mean seen across a parking lot, heard a rumor about, or saw on television. I mean a person with whom you have actually spent enough time to know as an individual.

I'm sure if you include only those individuals with whom you have had sustained and meaningful contact, you'll find that the number that conforms to your bias is very small. Sure, there may be someone who conforms, but that's because these inflexible beliefs have to have started somewhere. But just because your bias applies in some cases does not mean it applies to every member of that group.

To give you an idea of what I'm talking about, I remember a woman named Hannah who had a virulent bias that caused her to believe that all men are sexist. When she expressed that view to me during an interview, I immediately spotted it as a bias (that tiny word *all* is a dead giveaway) and asked her the only pertinent question: "How do you know that all men are sexist?"

Hannah's answer revealed the bad luck that, in her twenty-five-year career, she had been cursed with three male bosses who had blatantly sexist attitudes and management practices. Because her experience with these men was clearly emotionally intense, it is little wonder that a bias was born.

That's not to say that her attitude was logical—it wasn't. If we do some research and look at Hannah's experience separately from her understandably intense emotion, a peculiar picture emerges. My research revealed that, during Hannah's twenty-five-year career, there were approximately 125 million men who were of the age and profession to have been her boss. Now, I'm not saying that of those 125 million there weren't more sexist men than just Hannah's maligned 3, but still, to base an opinion upon experience with 3 out of 125 million people just doesn't make sense.

Now it's your turn. Let's see how well you do at bringing the evidence for your biases into logical perspective.

Antibias Activity: It's Who You Know

Pick one bias of which you are aware. Once you have identified the bias, use this space to list all the people you **really** know who actually conform to that inflexible belief. (I suspect it will be a very short list.)

THINK ABOUT HOW YOU'D FEEL

Empathy is one of the bigger guns in our bias-reduction arsenal. Studies out of the University of Iowa have shown that feeling empathy for those different from us can reduce bias and, if practiced consistently enough, even cut down the number of discriminatory acts.

Empathy is

the capacity for participating in or relating to another person's feelings.

The beauty of this bias-reduction strategy is that it isn't necessary that we fully understand what the other person is feeling. What we are after, and what we can realistically expect, is a reasonable grasp of the essence of his or her experience.

Take the able-bodied woman who is temporarily disabled by a broken leg. She will never feel the same amount of frustration experienced by a man permanently using a wheelchair. She can, however, approximate his emotion and thus feel enough empathy with this man and with others like him to reduce her bias against persons with disabilities.

Similarly, those of us who have never been blatantly discriminated against or passed up by a taxi because of the color of our skin can't fully grasp the pain and frustration those events can cause. But we can THINK back to times when we were rejected, ignored, or excluded and empathize to the extent needed to reduce our bias.

This is all great news, but the problem is that empathy does not always happen automatically. Sometimes we need to make a conscious effort to tap into these emotions. One way to facilitate this process is to deliberately ask ourselves questions like these:

1. How would I feel if I were in their situation?
2. If I were in their situation, how would I act and why?
3. Have I ever been in a situation even remotely similar to theirs? How did it make me feel? What did I do in response to those feelings?

Like WATCHING our first thoughts and assumptions about groups, feeling empathy is a matter of habit. The more we deliberately ask these empathy building questions, the more the answers will come to us automatically until, finally, empathy becomes a routine part of how we relate to others.

THINK ABOUT YOUR VALUES

Does your culture and organization value inclusion?

Is human equality a norm that permeated the messages you received growing up?

Are treating others with respect and giving them a fair chance things you value?

Most likely, the answer to each of these questions is a resounding "yes!" These values are probably so fundamental to how you live that you don't even get why I am asking questions about them.

It is these values that bring us to another principle of bias reduction that has been proven in study after study:

The more we THINK about the fact that our fundamental values do not fit with our biases, the less biased we are.

Weird, isn't it?

The idea here is that human beings are profoundly uncomfortable when asked to simultaneously hold opposing beliefs. This discomfort carries the fancy name of "cognitive dissonance."

Once we become aware that our beliefs don't fit together, cognitive dissonance kicks in, and the brain struggles to rid itself of the contradiction. Because many of our values are even more deeply rooted in our psyches than our biases, it is often the bias that makes for the door first.

So I invite you to take a hard look at the values you hold. They might be personal values or religious; they might have come to you through your family or community or via your own life choices. The source doesn't matter. What matters is this question:

Do those values fit with your biases, or on the other hand, are the two inconsistent and even contradictory?

THINK ABOUT PAUSING FOR A MOMENT

Let's face it: Unconscious biases have a nasty habit of popping up when we least expect them. And to make matters worse, this "popping up" is most apt to happen when we are the busiest. It's as if all the pressure and stress cause the more evolved brain to shut down and our more primitive and biased brain to come to life.

Fortunately, science reveals a solution to this problem that will make it easier for all of us to manage our biases. That solution involves, in fact, **not** THINKing. Well, I don't mean permanently—just long enough for our rational thoughts to rev up and override the unconscious. In other words,

Hit the pause button.

The power of the pause was explored by a psychologist named William Cunningham. Cunningham based his work on earlier studies that tracked the speed with which the alarm center of the brain spiked when subjects were shown faces of people who looked different from them.

This spike amounts to a primitive "jumping to conclusions" about the nature of people who are different. What Cunningham did was modify the previous research methodology just slightly. In the earlier studies, the faces were shown for only 30 milliseconds—removed so quickly that they could only be "seen" subconsciously. Cunningham decided to find out what would happen if the pictures were viewed for a longer period of time—525 milliseconds.

Although 525 milliseconds is still too brief for the conscious mind to grasp the image, the extended time was long enough to change the brain's response. Although there was still a spike when the faces appeared, it wasn't in the alarm center but instead in the part of the brain that controls rational thought.

The upshot—and the very good news—is this:

If given long enough, the conscious and rational brain has the ability to override even our most primitive biased impulses.

This explains why we tend to react with more bias when rushed to make quick decisions. There is simply no time for the rational brain to become engaged.

This conclusion sends a message that can help each and every one of us manage our biases. Let's get in the habit of taking a beat, a breath, or a moment even in the midst of the most extreme chaos and rush. That pause—that few seconds of delay—could be the difference between a biased decision and the ability to see people for who they really are.

Key #3

ACT

THE VIRTUE OF ACTING

Let's now move away from what is going on inside us, from things like WATCHing our thoughts and THINKing about the irrational origins of our biases. It's time to take ACTION. The ACTIONS we will talk about here include ACTING as if the bias does not exist and ACTING to identify what we have in common as a means of defeating bias.

ACT AS IF THE BIAS DOES NOT EXIST

Here's something that might surprise you: ACTING as if your bias does not exist is one of your most powerful antibias tools. With that in mind, does this ancient adage seem familiar?

Attitude follows behavior.

Aristotle figured that out way back in 300 BC, and it has been proven by behavior psychologists dozens of times since.

The principle that applies here is the same one discussed in the THINK chapter—cognitive dissonance. There we talked about the fact that human beings can't stand the psychological discomfort we experience when we try to hold opposing values in our minds (a bias and the value of equality, for example).

Here the dissonance sets in when we try to **believe** one thing (our bias) while at the same time **behaving** in a way that runs counter to that bias. When that happens, something has to give. If we work hard enough at keeping our behaviors out of line with our inflexible belief, the bias eventually begins to fade.

Besides cognitive dissonance, there's another reason that self-consciously ACTING in an unbiased way reduces bias. This has to do with the neural pathways in the brain that connect one part of this magnificent organ to another.

These pathways are formed in exactly the same way as the rut that runs in a muddy circle in my backyard. Unsightly as it is, I have affection for that rut because it was formed by the joyful running in circles of our two Labrador Retrievers. That rut is my yard's "neural pathway." Similarly, in the case of the brain, the pathways are formed and strengthened by repeated behaviors.

But what happens if the dogs decide one day to change their route? A new rut will form, and the original will gradually fill in until it virtually disappears. The same process applies to our brains. When we change our behaviors, the pathways begin to change. That change, in turn, makes the new—unbiased—behaviors easier and easier to execute. And through time and repetition, they become essentially automatic.

"ACTING" STEP BY STEP

At the start of this book, I asked, "Do you really want to take this on?" The reason for that question was that it takes courage to face our biases. I'm now calling on you to show another type of courage. What is needed here is the courage to look at past behaviors that might have reflected a biased attitude and make the commitment to change.

Take, for example, the courage shown by a team leader named Bess. Bess, although a good person, had a bias that seriously compromised her ability to do her job.

Ever since she could remember, Bess had, as she put it, a "thing" about people who couldn't express themselves well in English. Whether the reason was that English was their second language or that they lacked formal education, as soon as she heard them speak, Bess's mind was filled with judgments like "unintelligent," "will never be able to do the job" (even if the job has little to do with communication skills), "uncreative," and "doesn't have much to contribute."

Bess wasn't proud of these views and knew they didn't make sense. She also felt awful when one Latino employee complained that she was discriminating against him. The problem was, because of her upbringing and past experiences, Bess just couldn't seem to shake the bias—that is, until she learned about how the brain works and that if she ACTed as if her bias did not exist, it might just disappear.

So let's take Bess through this process of "ACTing as if." As the process unfolds, I encourage you to think of a bias of your own and see if you can figure out how you might ACT to defeat it by using this technique.

Before we get started, keep this in mind: The bias that you or Bess holds is tenacious and sneaky. It will do all it can to influence you to behave in a biased way. Because of this sneakiness, it is important that the new behaviors have these characteristics:

- Be specific ("I will say good morning every time I see this person," not "I will be more friendly").
- Be measureable ("I will do this three times a week," not "I will do it often").

- Be observable by yourself and others ("I will take notes when people speak up at meetings," not "I will listen more carefully").

With these parameters in mind, here is the account of Bess's journey.

Bess's Journey

Step 1: Bess identified one behavior that her bias was tricking her into doing.

> Biased Behavior: Bess realized that when the targets of her bias spoke at meetings, she didn't really listen to what they had to say. To make matters worse, she received feedback that her lack of attentiveness was obvious to the group.

Step 2: Bess then identified the negative consequences—for herself and others—of this behavior. The purpose of this step was to motivate Bess to make the change.

> Negative Consequences: By not hearing the ideas of everyone on her team, Bess risked missing out on creative approaches while simultaneously alienating individuals who might benefit both her and the company.

Step 3: The third step in Bess's journey grew naturally out of the first and second. She described specific, measureable, observable ACTIONS that ran directly counter to the biased behavior.

Bias-Free Behaviors

1. She asked each person who spoke at the meeting at least one respectful but probing follow-up question regarding his or her remarks. Not only did this commitment force Bess to listen so that she could formulate a pertinent question, it also demonstrated to the group that she was really paying attention.

2. She took notes on everyone's remarks. Again, the process of taking notes forced her to listen while showing others that she cared about what was being said.

Step 4: Bess then committed to engaging in these two behaviors consistently and for long enough to begin to weaken her bias.

Behavior Time Commitment: In Bess's case, because she had meetings once a week, she committed to engaging in these behaviors for three weeks in a row.

Step 5: Bess then observed the positive responses her new behaviors triggered in others.

The ultimate consequence of these changes in behavior was that Bess's bias began to fade. It faded for three reasons.

First, it faded because the dissonance (the incompatibility) between her bias-free behavior and her biased attitude subconsciously bothered Bess. The two could not cohabit the same person. Fortunately, in Bess's case, it was the bias that moved out first. Second, as Bess continued to behave differently, her brain gradually rewired itself to reflect both the new behaviors and the unbiased thoughts they spawned.

The third reason her bias faded was that it just couldn't survive the onslaught of positive and varied information that Bess's new behaviors caused to come her way. The better she treated people, the better they responded; the better they responded, the more positive her experience; the more positive her experience, the better she felt about a group that she had previously dismissed.

Try "ACTING as if"—it works.

ACT TO IDENTIFY AND CULTIVATE COMMON GROUND

Gay/straight, black/white, American/foreign national, man/woman, generation X/baby boomer—it sure seems to me we have a lot of language that refers to how we are different.

That's fine. Differences matter—they are to be respected and honored and valued. But we should also respect, honor, and value what we have in common. This is important for several reasons, not the least of which is this one:

The more we focus on commonalities, the less power our biases have to control our thoughts.

I'm not, of course, for one moment saying we stop valuing diversity—that would be a disaster. What I am saying is that it is time we begin to balance honoring difference with looking at what we have in common. These two attitudes are by no means incompatible, and in fact, we might think of them as two sides of the same inclusion coin.

HOW COMMON GROUND REDUCES BIAS

Identifying what we have in common reduces bias for a couple of reasons. First, once we identify commonalities, we no longer place our sole focus on how the other person is different and in turn on any inflexible beliefs we may associate with that difference.

If you think about it, this makes sense. When we look at how people are different—be it by race or age or culture or any other dimension of diversity—we automatically put characteristics on that difference. Those characteristics often become our biases. The upshot of this is that if we balance our focus on differences with attention to what we have in common, our biases have less to cling to and less reason to exist.

Looking for commonalities also reduces bias because human beings tend to like people with whom they have identified similarities. And it gets better: we also are fairer to those with whom we feel an affinity.

Taking all this into consideration, looking for what we have in common—while valuing diversity—simply makes bias-reducing sense. And that brings us to the ACTION needed to bring common ground into the fight against bias.

I do not grieve that I am not known; I grieve if I do not know others.

Confucius

REACH OUT TO PEOPLE DIFFERENT FROM YOU

This reaching out might mean sitting next to someone different in the cafeteria, stopping in the hall to have a conversation with a teammate whom you barely know, or joining a club whose members are from many diverse groups.

I know this seems like common sense, but there's more to it than just sitting down and having a conversation. In fact, there are several ways to make this contact particularly fruitful in terms of identifying common ground and, in turn, reducing bias.

First, if at all possible...

The contact should be relaxed and informal.

An unhurried tone is most conducive to the kind of interpersonal contact that will reveal shared values, needs, and interests.

Second, during your time together...

Ferret out shared interests.

Bring up subjects and ask questions that will reveal what you have in common. Perhaps you have a passion for baseball but never thought to bring that up with your blind colleague. You figured, after all, that because he can't see or play the game, he wouldn't be interested. If you talk about it, you might just discover that his favorite pastime is listening to games and that his knowledge of baseball statistics would put yours to shame. You'll never know until you have the conversation.

A third practice to keep in mind when reaching out is to...

Care about and notice what you have in common.

You'll know what I mean by "care about" if you recall the last time you were in the market for a new car. Maybe one criterion you had for the model you chose was that it be fairly unusual—that you don't often see it on the road. The snag in this criterion is that you may not see many of them before you decide on the model, but once you make the decision, they (much to your dismay) appear to be everywhere!

You wonder, *Where did all those cars suddenly come from?* In fact, it's not the number of automobiles that has changed but rather your attitude. Once you began to care about that model, it became forefront in your thinking and no longer blended in with every other vehicle on the freeway. These heightened observation skills happen because of a fundamental truth of how the mind works: we notice what we care about.

Just like with that particular model of car, if we care about the common ground that all human beings share, we will begin to notice shared values, interests, needs, and concerns in every relationship we cultivate. You'll be amazed at what you begin to see.

Antibias Activity: The Three/Two/One Process

The Three/Two/One Process facilitates the identification of what we have in common with people whom we normally think of as very different from us. It consists of the following steps:

Step #1: Make contact with **three** people whom you do not know well and whom you believe to have different values and interests from your own.

Step #2: Talk to each of those people about **two** subjects that you might, in the past, have felt would not interest them.

Step #3: On the basis of the commonalities you discover, identify **one** of these people as someone you might like to get to know better.

FINALLY: FEEL

Defeating bias is, as you've seen, quite a journey: from Watching so we can gain awareness of our own biases, to weakening biases by managing what we Think, to Acting to defeat them altogether. And of course, there is also what we all hope to feel. We hope to…

Feel good about our willingness to uncover unconscious biases;

Feel empathy for the experiences of others;

Feel respect for people different from us;

Feel good about the positive responses that our new attitudes and behaviors inspire;

Feel proud of our commitment to valuing diversity while identifying common ground; and finally

Feel good about everything we do to overcome bias.

As you can see, whether your focus is on defeating bias so you will see the world more clearly or to benefit others, your hard and courageous work is well worth the effort.

Appendix

THE QUESTION GAME

Of the many ways to defeat unconscious bias, identifying what we have in common is perhaps the most powerful. For that reason, I have included here an activity designed to bring to light the commonalities shared by people of otherwise diverse backgrounds. Consisting of a list of questions followed by discussion, these instructions for facilitating this process are simple:

1. Invite a volunteer to function as the "primary responder" to the questions you supply. If time allows for more than one person to be the responder, try to achieve as much visible diversity as possible among those chosen for this role.
2. Select five questions from the list. As you ask each question out loud, have both the primary responder and the rest of the group write down their answers. (Depending upon the time allotted and the size of the group, the number of questions asked can be increased or decreased.)
3. After all the questions are asked, have the primary responder provide his or her answers, one by one.
4. After each response is read, ask the group if any of their answers are similar to those provided by the primary responder.

If so, have them share the details. At every opportunity, make the point that we have a lot more in common than we realize. This point is particularly powerful if the two people who answered similarly are in other ways very different from each other.

5. Encourage participants, once they return to the workplace, to build on the commonalities that this activity has brought to light.

Think of these questions as mere suggestions. Use your imagination and experience to add more to the list.

1. What single nonliving item would you rescue from a fire in your home and why?
2. If you could have had any occupation other than your own, what would it be? What is it about that job that appeals to you?
3. If given a million dollars to spend freely, what would you spend it on? Why would you make that choice?
4. If you could have lunch one-on-one with any person, living or dead, that you currently do not know, who would it be and why?
5. What three pieces of advice did your parents give you? Have you found that advice valuable?
6. What do you remember most fondly about your favorite holiday or tradition? Provide details.
7. If you could live during any time in history, when would it be and why?
8. What one item, other than a boat, would you take to a deserted island and why?
9. What talent that you don't currently possess would you most like to have? What is it about that talent that appeals to you?
10. What about you or your achievements are you most proud?

ABOUT THE AUTHOR

D r. Sondra Thiederman is a leading expert on workplace diversity/inclusion and unconscious bias reduction. For twenty-five years, she has sustained a reputation as a speaker and facilitator who involves audiences while expertly leading them on a journey to greater awareness of how to function successfully in our increasingly diverse and inclusive workplaces.

The recipient of a doctorate with an emphasis on cross-cultural studies from UCLA, Sondra has served as consultant to the University of California and on the Diversity Cabinet of the American Red Cross. She is currently an expert panelist for O'Mara and Richter's *Global Diversity and Inclusion Benchmarks*.

Sondra's work is featured in several training videos including *Gateways to Inclusion* and *Is It Bias?* She is also the author of five books, including *The Diversity and Inclusion Handbook*, published by The Walk the Talk Company.

Sondra welcomes your comments and can be contacted via her website: www.thiederman.com.

DIVERSITY/INCLUSION
RESOURCES

To learn more about Sondra's products—including bulk discount copies of this handbook—or to inquire about her speaking and customized webinars, simply contact us by phone at 619-583-4478 or by e-mail at stphd@thiederman.com, or visit www.thiederman.com.

Made in the USA
Columbia, SC
28 August 2020